Count Edweird Lefang's

Rhymin' Halloween

Count Edweird Lefang's

Rhymin' Halloween

by

Eddie Morales

Contents

Introduction

After having completed two books of poetry of a more serious nature, *A Reason for Rhyme* and *The Suicide Sonnets*, I thought it was time for a book of rhyming poetry that would be more fun than serious, or at least of a topic that could be fun *and* serious.

A few years ago, I wrote for a Halloween poetry recital several limericks which went over well. Afterwards, I thought it would be nice to have a book of poetry with Halloween as the theme. Well, first I went to the bookstore to see what types of books were available on this theme and found much of the poetry more for the younger audience. There weren't any books made for teenagers or adults in this area, so I went to the Internet. I searched once more for Halloween poetry, and again I found most of the poetry was for young children.

Taking it one step further, I looked for Halloween poems by famous poets, and I found a few, but not much. Most of my searches brought up the same poets and poems.

Some of these poems were, *The Apparition* by John Donne; *A Dream Within a Dream, The Haunted Palace, Dreamland,* and *The Bells* by Edgar Allan Poe; *Because I Could Not Stop For Death* by Emily Dickinson; *the Cambridge ladies who live in furnished souls* by e.e. cummings; *Ghost House* by Robert Frost; *The Ghost of a Flower* by Anonymous; *Halloween* by

Robert Burns; *The Haunted Oak* by Paul Laurence Dunbar; and not much else.

Of course, we can't forget the three witches around the cauldron in Shakespeare's play *Macbeth,* and their *Double, double toil and trouble; / Fire burn, and caldron bubble.* I'm sure I left many good poets and poems out, but basically there wasn't much. Finally, I went to the online bookstores and bought numerous digital books on the subject of Halloween, and I was disappointed.

So, I decided to write my own book of Halloween poetry, and I wanted to adhere to the rhyming forms. In addition, I wanted to write a book of Halloween poetry that could be used in a classroom setting, illustrating many of the different rhyming forms that exist, and have the poems be entertaining to the student as well, as they went about learning about the different rhyming forms.

Hopefully, I have succeeded in doing just that, and made it both, fun and educational.

You Are Horrorfully Invited

Hear you one! Hear you two! Hear you ALL!
Count Lefang's having a Halloween Ball.
Bring your family, bring your friends.
The mayhem won't stop 'til the moonlight ends!

Enter you monsters, demons, and wraiths,
Through Devil's Garden the graveyard waits!
Come all you ghosts, come all you ghouls,
Come the werewolf who howls and drools!

We've things that wriggle, things that crawl,
Things that climb up the ivied walls;
Things that hang from their spidery webs,
And things that slither beneath your beds!

Beware the warlock and witches too,
They've come to mix their potions for you.
With hexes and charms they will cast a spell
To open the gates to the fires of Hell.

Now bring your family, bring your friends,
The mayhem won't stop 'til the moonlight ends!
So come you one, come you two, come you ALL!
And see if you live through his Halloween Ball!

Count Lefang's Chant Royal

He was born the night when all warlocks ride
On the wings of hate, with all of their might;
With nowhere to run, and nowhere to hide,
With shield in his left and sword in his right,
Lefang, on the battlefield, braced to wait
For the Warlock Krone, with the face oblate;
"Stand fast!" yelled Count Lefang, words to obey,
As the warlocks fell with their swoop and sway
And dropped like a storm on a grayish heath;—
And there they stood, with their mettle at play,
All face to face with the demons of death.

They dug in their heels, and anchored their pride,
Standing shoulder to shoulder, Knight by Knight;
The warlocks dared swordplay, and they complied,
As Count Lefang roared, "For our souls we fight!"
Upon Lefang's shield came a heavy weight,—
'Twas Warlock Krone, with his red, hairless pate,
Nails like cold steel, and dark flesh in decay;
Krone hissed, "You are mine!" Lefang thundered,
"Nay!"
And with conjuring, Krone gained height and breadth
To test the Knight, and Lefang, no delay,
Stood face to face with that demon of death.

Lefang failed surrender, and woe betide
The Knight who gives in to creatures of night.
He prayed for his soul, and God Krone defied,
So he lunged then forth, this demon to smite.
With stench so foul, and his visage irate,

4

Krone came upon him with daggers of hate,
As he bellowed, "You'll pay, Lefang, you'll pay!"
Lefang knew well how a wolf loves its prey,
But he was not ready for stone and wreath,
And anew, Lefang, with valiant display,
 Stood face to face with that demon of death.

Then Warlock Krone raged, "I won't be denied!"
And Lefang spewed back, "Die you *here* tonight!"
His shield split Krone's face, his sword slit him wide,
But from Krone's flesh sprang a sulfurous blight;
And there they struggled in the hands of Fate,
While from Krone's blood, as through some hellish gate,
Arose ten demons with fangs in array;
Too many they were to keep them at bay,
And one pierced his neck, with foulest of breath.
When he'd slain them all, he kneeled down to pray,
There, face to face with those demons of death.

That demonic Krone more evil he plied,
And with dying breaths, he cursed with delight,
"You're damned, Count Lefang, to the darker side;
You'll soon enough join the creatures of fright.
You'll die-not-die by this hex I create,
To live with a thirst you will never sate!
So your blood, drop by drop, will dry away,
And you'll seek it out by the lack of day!
Forever the night to you I bequeath!"
Once more Lefang stood, as Hell had its way,
There, face to face, with that demon of death.

Lefang's wound was dire, never to abate
And was knightly buried in his estate;
But the curse inside him led him astray,
And he rose from the ground with hunger great;
With the stars above, and hell underneath,
Were all to look at him, they'd surely say:
Lefang has the face of a demon of death!

Lefang's Lie in a Lai
Your blood was divine!
Better than red wine,
It's true.
Hence, I crossed the line
When I chose to dine
On you.
But know, I will pine; —
For making you mine,
I'm blue.

Lefang's Vampire Dreams

I lie down within my coffin,
Daylight out, my time for sleeping;
There I dream, as I do often,
People weeping, weeping, weeping.

I dream of folks so free and wild,
And how I've got no time to waste;
They soon forget how well they smiled,
Before my urges carved a taste.

How warm the blood, my ecstasy,
How down the neck it trickles so;
A tiny river flows for me,
A red bouquet of love I know.

My passion overrides my sin,
So I must feast until the death,
And heaven feeds my hell within
Until it leaves us out of breath.

Oh, I must dream, and dream again,
For Time the night must also keep,
And when I wake, I love it when
The living weep, and weep, and weep.

A Roundel to My Fangs

I love to bite, as sure as Death has not a care, or thing to
fear,
With such a passion, I forget myself, as if in trance, with
such delight,
That I am cast to heaven, though from hell you'll hear me
hiss and cheer,
I love to bite!

No fire compares in brightness, not the stars, or moon in
full at night,
To the impassioned smile I there display, aquake,
beneath your ear,
In scarce control of what I seek, and you provide with all
my might.

It is your pulse that beats my seething drums, the invite
that I hear!
How can I fail my nature's call, the panic in your nervous
fright?
So moves my soul, and you will know, though I can never
shed a tear,
I love to bite.

A Virelai Nouveau On Being a Vampire

Your nature is your nature, so it goes,
And nature to a vampire's all he knows.
He cannot help his urgency for night,
For then is when his neediness best flows.
The dead know well the dark, the living light;
Whatever dies, dies, whatever grows, grows,
Your nature is your nature, so it goes.

One hears of horrors, or of tales of woes,
But inner temper's how the rooster crows,
Unless such creature dies of wound or fright.
It's always hard to keep at bay your foes,
But conflict seems to be an earthly plight.
One must embrace the temperament one shows,
And nature to a vampire's all he knows.

So if one day, you two should come to blows,
You may not win, though vicious be your fight.
For nature to a vampire's all he knows,
And nature is your nature, so it goes.

Lefang's Warning in a Virelai

Many men have tried,
And many men have died,
Looking for me.
So swallow here your pride,
Such folly's merely suicide.
Let it go, let me be.
Don't go looking for where I reside,
For certainly, we will collide
In one grandiose atrocity.

Better to be blind, not see
What death will most assuredly
Place before his knell.
You'll hear it ring, repeatedly,
Again, again, so wickedly,
To call you into hell.
Don't be a fool, go on, and flee,
Make your haste across the sea.
Or else, I'll heed the knelling bell!

But if you must, I here foretell,
Things your way will not go well,
So make your peace, and now decide.
See your kin and say farewell,
Knowing they have perished well,
And bury those for whom you've cried.
This is your last, I've naught to sell,
Seek not again the place I dwell,
For many men have tried, and died.

Count Lefang's Dilemma

I've been stymied by my studies,
And I've asked this of my buddies:
What can ever drive a gentleman insane?

Their odd responses, it appears,
Keep their senses in arrears,
And no two of them may ever be the same.

Some take to piercings of the nose,
While others fixate on the toes,
And I find myself an utter, nervous wreck,

Because there's nothing more spectacular
Than one fat, juicy jugular
And that, my friend, is why I love the neck.

A neck is slick, a neck is cool,
A neck will cause my mouth to drool.
If I see one it will stir my hunger pangs.

And I can't be held responsible
For something so delectable
It floods my very essence through my fangs.

Necks, necks, necks—
They are everywhere I go.
Necks, necks, necks—
Set my icy eyes aglow.

Necks, necks, necks—
Where all I ever need to know
Is necks, necks, necks
Is where the crimson fluids flow.

Oh, how sweetly don't they beckon!
Oh, I'll take them all, I reckon!
By the bushel or the peck!
Oh, I'll make them all a wreck!

Oh, no drops will I ever leave behind,
Not a speck!
And the method I may use is
Hunt-and-peck!

And as I've said, a neck is cool,
A neck will cause my mouth to drool,
And I cannot keep my bloody urge in check!

Oh, what the heck!
Oh what the heck!
Oh what the heck, heck, heck, heck,
Heck, heck, heck, heck,
HECK!

I LOVE THE NECK!

Count Lefang's Bloody Alliterisen

So sweet and tender, necks are nifty things,
For jugulars, beneath, bring joy, and my heart sings
With icy inclination; warmed with
Blood, a vampire's verve, and flesh, is kin and kith
To those who give, who gave, and died.
I love the lost, and I am pale with pride;—
I'm glad you'll give your blood, your last, to me.

Don't think the worst if you are truly pure,
For swiftly to your kin your presence I'll assure;
And if they give you grace, you will not
Suffer long, save for a sting, so soon forgot.
Turn your head aside, hail yourself,
For I am doomed, and cannot help myself,
But glad you'll give your blood, your last, to me.

Count Lefang's Going Bats

Delightful creatures are my bats,
Especially the vampire kind,
And why they are, by folks, maligned
Is odd, for unlike dogs and cats,
They neither drool nor shred the mats.
I never need to raise some hell
For what they drop, or for the smell;
My furniture is safe and sound,
Should ever I not be around,
So by my bats, I think they're swell.

So much like me, they dream by day,
While I, in coffin, sleep at ease,
Until the light wanes by degrees,
And sun to dusk has given way
To call my creatures out to play.
When I am caught up in the spell,
As if by sounding of a bell,
I stir from sleep, and they do too,
As if to say, I welcome you;
They are my bats, I think they're swell.

And out they go, in wondrous flight,
With air beneath their leath'ry wings,
Intent on finding savory things,
Underneath the veil of night.
Oh, folks may run with nervous fright,
For all will hear from Death his knell,
And from the fear,—the smell, the smell!
Aroma irresistible!

Such corpuscles delectable!
They are my bats, I think they're swell.

Then from my coffin I will rise
With hunger like the night before,
And from my cellar I will soar
To join my comrades in the skies.
I'll hear folks scream, and hear their cries,
But nothing will their fears dispel,
Because I know the fires of hell,
And if I let them rise from death,
They'll say with every ounce of breath,
Now we're all bats, and we are swell!

Count Lefang's Rondeau to Blood

Blood! Fluid essence of the human store—
Redolent in its sweet bouquet,
To make head swoon and the body sway!
Ah! To sip it lightly, and crave it more,
This crimson nectar, which I adore!
I need it now and without delay—
Blood!

The tender necks, into which I bore,
So drench my fangs, and I lap away
The jugular's juice, without delay,
And for a moment, I quench my thirst for—
BLOOD!

If Looks Could Kill

If looks could kill, I'd tell you lies,
To keep those daggers in your eyes.
I wouldn't trust your wicked smile,
Your temper hot, your fiendish guile,
Your homicidal tendencies.

I'd use deceit, and any guise,
To keep myself from my demise;
To wit, I would not stay awhile,
If looks could kill.

For if I stay, who'd hear my cries?
My corpse would surely feed the flies.
Your discourse could my "self" revile,
But if I run, I'd foil the trial,
So I'd not tarry, being wise,
If looks could kill!

The Less Pay Shew Stone

Oh, erudite and sacred stone, awake!
Reveal to me, here what I ask of you,
And lead my mind to visions that are true,
So I may know here forth what path to take!

I'm Séla Romé, I hear and I wake!
No words here be spoken, vile and untrue,
Your mind will be cleared, all thoughts into view,
But caution for whatever sins you make!

Count Lefang's having a Halloween Ball;
I need a handbag and shoes for tonight.
If I don't look bad, I won't go at all!

Oh, Darrrlinnk! Go to Horrorstein's & Fright!
They've got ghastly bags and shoes to enthrall,
And you'll win "Worst Dressed" on Halloween night!

A Ghostly Villanelle

From the world of spirits come the unseen dead,
With feet that make no sound upon the floors;
Wistful shadows, by their earthly errands sped,

Who may by day, or by the light of the moon, head
Across a sea of stones, maybe the heaths, and moors,
That may so link the world of the living with the dead.

To and fro, they come and go, led
by necessity to walk through walls and doors,
Shadowy shapes, who are, by their earthly errands, sped.

By the gate, by the fireplace, by the side of your bed,
They wait and watch, then tend their chores,
These gossamer phantoms, these residents of the dead.

They are the senseless who, by the substantial fed,
Are bound to linger from here to distant shores,
As spectral apparitions by their earthly errands sped.

And all be warned, by their words unsaid,
Mind the presence of the ghost that soars
From the world of spirits, the land of unseen dead,
These wistful shadows on their earthly errands sped.

Count Dracula

Count Dracula ordered Bacardi,
One night at a Halloween party;
Didn't like it, then bit,
Someone's throat he had slit,
To make Bloodied Rum smooth and hearty.

Werewolf

The Wolf Man is really a cretin
When kids come around Trick-or-treatin';
Toothed all he could take,
Got a bad stomach ache,
From all of the brats he had eaten.

Mummy

The Mummy thinks he's so entrapping,
With all of his threads overlapping;
Thinks he's God's gift to ghouls,
But his ghoul overrules:
"You can't judge a gift by its wrapping!"

Frankenstein

Now Frankenstein's looks may be jolting,
And won't stop the ladies from bolting;
But from both of his bolts,
You get ten-thousand volts,
And when he's not charged—he's revolting!

Bride of Frankenstein

The Frankenstein Bride's in a tizzy,
And staggers around drunk and dizzy.
From his two shiny bolts
Frankie's ten-thousand volts,
Has spiked her hair up, burnt and frizzy.

Ghoul

The Ghouls are all monsters revulsive,
With appetites crude and repulsive;
For when kids Trick-or-treat,
It's the kids they will eat,
Which *I* find obsessive-compulsive!

Ghost

The Ghost has a pale predilection,
For testing all forms of detection;
See you will, see you won't,
Now you see, now you don't—
But I see right through his deception!

Goblin

The Goblin is sure to be creeping
Inside of your house when you're sleeping;
Likes to kick Kitty Kat,
Bang old Duke with a bat,
And scare all the kids 'til they're weeping!

Scarecrow

The Scarecrow is often maltreating
The children who come Trick-or-treating;
Thought he'd treat them to fright,
But they tricked him one night,
And took all his stuffing for eating.

Gremlin

A Gremlin's a gruesome mechanic,
With standard and kids automatic,
Halloween is his life,
And with wrench and a knife,
He whacks them 'til they run erratic.

Grim Reaper

The Reaper is grim and mysterious.
To meet him is really quite serious.
Halloween is to dread,
Now his guests are all dead,
For scything's a cut deleterious!

Dr. Jekyll and Mr. Hyde

Doc Jekyll makes quite a commotion
When mixing a volatile potion.
Once the tonic's inside
Out explodes Mister Hyde,
Who kills with a doubled devotion.

Warlock

The Warlock wields magic demonic;
On pitchfork he flies supersonic.
Down he'll dive with a treat,
That the kids love to eat,
To render them all catatonic.

Witch

The Witch is quite ugly and sloven;
And thirteen of them make a coven.
They get help for a spell
From the demons of hell,
To bake Cookie-Kids in an oven.

The Skeleton

The Skeleton's footsy and handy
When stealing the Halloween candy;
But the kids got their dibs
On his twenty-two ribs,
And Fido thinks bones are just dandy.

The Crypt Keeper

The Crypt Keeper's wild and rampageous,
With breath foul and highly contagious.
"Hello, kiddies!" he drools,
"If you stay, boils and ghouls,
I'll kill you with laughter outrageous!"

Jack-o-Lantern

Now Jack is a scary old Lumpkin
Who's carved out for being a bumpkin.
They scooped all his insides,
To make great tasting pies,
Which makes him one unlucky pumpkin!

Jack the Ripper

The Ripper has quite an attraction
For seeking a lady's reaction;
With no ifs ands or buts,
He will cut out her guts,
Then thank her for his satisfaction.

Wraith

The Wraith is a pale apparition
Who comes to avenge his condition.
All who still have a life
Will all come to great strife,
For Halloween's ripe for this mission.

Zombie

A Zombie's a lifeless man eater,
In search of a live trick-or-treater.
So on Halloween night
It's your body he'll bite,
And gulp down your blood by the liter.

Miss "Spider Killer" Muffett

Don't ever trust Little Miss Muffett,
And better look under her tuffett.
I'm quite sure that she hides
Gallons of pesticides,
So spiders will all have to rough it!

Mad Little Bo Peep

That Little Bo Peep is a harpy,
Connivingly shrewd and a sharpie.
Though, to give her some props,
All her lambs are lamb chops
She's grilling right now on the barbie.

Little Red Riding Hoodlum

That Little Red Riding Hood's mental,
To know her is quite detrimental.
The Wolf didn't do it,
The hunters all knew it,
Killed Grandma, then claimed, "accidental."

Homicidal Goldilocks

Now, Goldilocks never liked porridge,
And never went outside to forage;
No! Her mind was all set!
What she wanted to get
Were three bearskin coats now in storage.

The Murder of Ravens
(My sequel to "The Raven" in honor of Edgar Allan Poe)

While my sorrow kept me weeping, Time stepped up his
painful creeping,
'Till the chariot of Apollo swept o'er the Night's
Plutonian shore!
And the Raven, never flitting, on the bust of Pallas
sitting,
Like a viper, venom spitting, struck me once more to the
core!
Oh, how he made me shudder, the Raven o'er my
chamber door—
Still insisting: "Nevermore!"

But the nightmare mist departed, leaving mind and ear
unclouded,
And I heard a song that started from beneath the tufted
floor.
I began raving and ranting—like a banshee, wildly
panting!
I felt nothing more enchanting than the voice of sweet
Lenore!
"Come to me!" I shrieked, "fair maiden, whom the angels
name Lenore!
Mute the Raven's, 'Nevermore!'"

Then a voice, like some bright candle, burned, "Take
pistol by the handle,
And blast! that wretched demon sitting just above thy
chamber door!

Leave no evidence whatever he sat there like blackened leather,
Traces leave thee, not one feather, of that brazen bird of yore!
Pluck the life, like feathers plucked are, from that brazen bird of yore!
Quash the Raven's, 'Nevermore!'"

(Hark!) A deeper voice erupted, from some depth not yet corrupted,
And alarmingly instructed: (Leave well the pure and chaste Lenore!
Do not seek to make un-sainted, by this deed, so vile and tainted,
That which God so brightly painted, pressing doom to split thy door!
Grim and grave are plots engraved upon the Night's Plutonian shore!
Heed the Raven's, "Nevermore!").

Here the Raven, bird and devil, raised the note another level,
By pouring sanguinary evil o'er that one word I abhor!
"Prophet!" said I, "falsely praying!—death's a deadly game worth playing!
Keep thy blackened blood from spraying o'er my bust and chamber door!
Perch off the pallid bust of Pallas just above my chamber door!"
My Raven dared, "Nevermore!"

Then, the voice, with fiercer goading, set my flaming mind exploding!
Too, I dared not stop, and loaded lead and heart into the war;
While my maiden's song climbed higher, stared I red Raven-eyes of fire,
And heard a deeper voice suspire, (Now, doomed thou art, forevermore).
Still, the Raven, blasted Raven! that one last word did outpour!
The Raven croaked, "Nevermore!"

Settled by the madness broken, echoed I that last word spoken:
"Nevermore," said I, "dark token, from the Night's Plutonian shore,
Shall thy bolted beak torment me, or thy breast and breath present me,
With the word that now hath sent thee to the shadows on my floor.
Hallowed art thou, King of Shadows, by ebon hollows on my floor,
Longing for thy, 'Nevermore.'

"Fleeing sharp and cruel master lent thee far greater disaster,
When steadfast, Fate followed faster than thy wings could e'er outsoar!
From the east, now hear my Maiden, from within the distant Aidenn,
Balm she brings for me to bathe in 'til I feel the pain no

more.
And the melody Fate guides now is the song of sweet
Lenore!
Where croaks now thy, 'Nevermore?'"

Question asked, reply is certain—burning through each
purple curtain,
Sun's light fired all and paled the ebon shadows on my
floor!
Like the thunder, Lenore chanted, while the Maelstrom
puffed and panted,
And my bones were newly planted in the horrors I once
bore!
Bone for bone, one must atone, and I alone my terrors
bore!
There, I whispered, "Nevermore."

Hammered by the hellish howling, grander demons felt I
prowling,
Waiting, sniffing, drooling—growling! for the flesh my
neck bones wore!
Though my mind the worst kept fearing, from my
window I stood peering,
Keeping eyes upon the clearing, seeking sight of sweet
Lenore!
Amidst the sea of marble stones—peering back stood
sweet Lenore.
Then, I cried out, "Nevermore!"

Startled by this vile word spoken, somehow, found I, my
voice broken.

"Doubtless," thought I, "what I uttered, came from
weathered voice made sore!"
"Corvus! Darling!" called my maiden! "Say 'tis true you
come to Aidenn!
Ever shall we be and bathe in Gilead's balm
forevermore?"
Here I tried to make reply and tell her, "Yes—
forevermore!"
 Instead I cried, "Nevermore!"

Then, from beyond the marble sea, a thousand voices r-r-
rocked for me,
And plied my maiden's agony, so twisted in the face she
wore!
Greater pain my mind fermented, while that word Lenore
lamented,
Knowing well my voice had sent it, and still I tried to
speak once more!
I gathered deeper voice, to clear my voice—save! my
voice once more!
Again I cried, "Nevermore!"

A thousand voices r-r-rocked for me, and from beyond the
marble sea,
A plume, as black as black can be, rose high above the
stone laced shore;
But 'twas no plume released that day, 'twas plumage
from a higher sway,
Sent out to right, without delay, the blood I spilled
moments before.
And while Lenore, "Oh, Corvus!" cried, I bid adieu to

30

sweet Lenore,
By crying out, "Nevermore!"

An Angel, with that word, alit beside the angel Life once
writ,
And with Nepenthe's light relit the grimly, gravely
pained Lenore!
The three-tier-wingéd Seraph drew Lenore into its arms
and flew
Into a sky of heaven-blue, high above the stone-laced
shore!
While then I prayed Lenore forget, once high above the
stone-laced shore,
I ever said, "Nevermore!"

Anew, the voices r-r-rocked for me, and from above the
marble sea,
Each puff of plume slid down to see restored the Night's
Plutonian shore!
Like a canvas, feather tainted, puffs of plume the blue
repainted,
With a sorrow well acquainted with the darkness my soul
wore!
But no darkness could e'er blacken my bright vision of
Lenore!
Though I'd see her, nevermore!

While gliding o'er the marble sea, again the voices r-r-
rocked for me,
And from my window I did see a thousand ravens o'er
Night's shore!
One by one, with flirt and flutter, every tree they sought
to clutter,
While I pondered how to utter, "Please forgive me, sweet
Lenore!"
But well I knew that word from hell, and thought
instead, forevermore,
To torment her, nevermore!

Again, the ravens r-r-rocked for me—from every ghastly,
purple tree!
And a thousand pairs of eyes of red lit up the frightening
shore!
But I feared nothing, black or red! for Death cannot the
dead un-bed!
And 'twas the living word I said that brought to me my
sweet Lenore!
And the one soul I adore! shall fly with angels, evermore!
She flies!—so freed by, "Nevermore!"

And still the ravens r-r-rock for me, while here I rock
eternally,
For I am King! of all the shadows on the Night's
Plutonian shore!
And should you gaze into my eyes, therein a radiant
maiden flies,
With no memory that my cries are all for her—my love
Lenore.

And her love shall light my sorrow, morrow after morrow, and evermore.
I shall forget her—"NEVERMORE!"

Ode to My Ghoulfriend

Oh Damsel, flesh so fresh we both have known,
Let us share this love, and therein call our own;
For sure, your soul, is now enmeshed with mine—
To you, the corpse, to me the crimson wine!
The bloody ale will flow from necks I strike,
And from the drained remains, do what you like.
We burn the flame which both our urges drive:
To seek the flesh which keep our souls alive.
Align with me, along the tomb-stoned place,
To keep those blackened eyes upon your face.
I'll keep them ripe! to your abundant store,
And each depletion will then see ten more!
Your nature will provide, to keep you young,
As does the scarlet mead upon my tongue.
We'll shun the day, and beg the moon to shine
Upon your rabid visage, pure, divine.
You noble creature, you unholy maid,
Will find the poets by your looks betrayed.
These generous fruits, gathered in their prime,
Will show your quickness and maturing time.
One hail and hardy more, you'll have your fill,
But rest until I've had my bloody spill;
For I will tread where hapless souls abound,
Each dark and gloomy night, so long as you're around.

A Pantoum For the Wrong Twin

If only I had murdered you instead of her,
I would now be happy with your foul and evil twin,
Preying on delectables the world can offer,
Instead of trying to save this wretched world from sin.

I would have been joyous with your foul and evil twin;
Her sweet irreverence for life would now be mine.
Instead of trying to save this wretched world from sin,
We'd sink our teeth into the flesh of human swine.

Her sweet impiety for life would now be mine
Had I not chosen hastily, not sure which witch was
which;
I tore her like I would the flesh of human swine,
To suffer later, and find, I lost my soul-mate witch.

Had I not wrongly chosen, not sure which witch was
which,
We'd now be preying on delectables the world has to
offer;
But now I suffer, for I've lost my soul-mate witch,
Because I failed to murder you instead of her.

The Grim Reaper

My scythe is long and sharp, of moonlit shine,
First forged before the first of souls was cast,
Then unto me was placed the task, divine,
To reap from one until the very last.
I neither ravage nor a kingdom build,
But from the Earth, I take each leaf and bough
At time when Winter's breath has blown and chilled,—
For when your time is now, your time is now.

I've not, like One, the elevated brow,
But in the end, I am the one real truth;—
For whether high, enthroned, or hitched to plough,
Of proper ebb of life, or new of youth,—
Of wretchedness, or highest in your grace,
No aberration turns me from my vow,
When last the moment comes to show my face;
For when your time is now, your time is now.

So come with me, and rest on Earth your fears,
Succumb, as do the floating leaves of fall,
To walk the path of never ending years;
It is prescribed, by Law, to one and all,
And never influenced by love or hate;
Be gallant, poised, and take your final bow;—
I've not a plaint with you, not one to wait,
And if your time is now, your time is now.

Beneath Your Bed

Above me, you lie sound asleep,
Beforehand having counted sheep,
While in the night, I hiss your name,
And wait to start my creeping game.
I think about your fleshy charms,
Your supple neck, and tasty arms,
That my fangs drool of things to come,
 And I can't wait to slither from
beneath your bed.

I hear you moan, I hear you start,
The nightmare spurs your racing heart;
I crawl your way while you complain,
My eager wish, to give you pain
Which, by my fangs, I know you feel.
Then all my glory I reveal,
With bite and tentacles you fear,
And it's too late, we disappear—
beneath your bed!

The Deadly Rose

What mystery has captured my fair Rose
That all my happiness has turned to woes?
Though all her life from earth was shortly clipped,
It seems she stirs, and begs release from crypt.
A fathom keeps her still, but is she deep
Enough to keep me sane, and sound of sleep?
Her piercing screams reach far within my mind;
Her implorations for me to be kind
Is not of one whose taken ill and dies,
But surely one, who by the dusk, will rise.
She calls me nigh, and I so crave it so,
But for her sake, and love, I must not go.
However, she is strong, and I am weak,
That I am losing ground, and long to seek
Her out, so I may see her face and kiss
Again her lips, of sweet and tender bliss.
I pray, entomb me near her wretched bed
As well; though I am living, better dead
Than I be damned along, and lose my soul.
She calls, and calls, and I fear lose control!
Oh, yet she calls, and calls, and calls again!
No peace of mind is mine, not ever, when
I feel the pain of all her loneliness.
If only I could free Rose from her stress,
But I am bound in jacket, tight and straight.
Much better that our love convert to hate,
For never will she see the blue of sky
Anew, and that is reason well I die.
She calls once more, with wild and frantic blows,

That I do suffer for my lovely Rose.
Do keep me bound, or else I will reply,
For though she demon be, I will comply.
I'll seek and find her wicked stone and wreath,
And free my deadly Rose who lies beneath!

Coven Round the Cauldron

Let a black cat walk around
A twelve and one foot circled ground;
When the circle is complete,
It's time to give the cauldron heat.
Light the fire and feed the flame,
So to the pot you do the same!
Thirteen witches round the pot,
Must now cast in their filthy lot.

Witch 1
As I stir this cauldron, to and fro,
In these poisoned guts must go!
By ingestion, indigestion, feel the pain,
Until they go indeed insane!

Witch 2
A heart of stone, a chicken bone—
I stir until three times I stir;
The silken ladies will grow fur,
All while the moon has come and gone!

Witch 3
Round and round the cauldron go—
An eyeless frog, a headless bat!
Round and round the cauldron go—
A glob of dung, and baby fat!
Nuts the good folk round they go!
▯

Witch 4
Warts from a wild boar's rump,
Fleas from a camel's hump,
Fungi from a rotten stump,
A six-inch louse, bloody plump,
Keeps them squirming, makes them jump!

Witch 5
In the cauldron boil and bake,
A dead man's toe, a garter snake,
The purple pus of putrid eel,
To make the bravest snort and squeal!

Witch 6
From my nose I give you snot—Flooey!
Ahem, ahem, from my throat my phlegm—Thooey!
Gives them rot, the lot of them! —Flooey! Thooey!

Witch 7
From my lungs I give my breath,
From my belly vomit too—
For a plague from out this stew of death!

Witch 8
Half a dozen lips of yak,
Licked by my own tongue,
Dipped in sweat from an old sow's back,
To make them wheeze and up a lung!
⬚

Witch 9
My own knickers,
Soiled and wet,
Makes familiar
Of a pet.

Witch 10
Cobra's rattle, and hornet's sting,
Chameleon's leg, and dragonfly's wing, —
Placed inside a pillow cover,
Craves a demon for a lover!

Witch 11
With these black nails from my toes,
Something wicked in there goes;
By this mandrake's fleshy thumbs,
Something evil this way comes!

Witch 12
I'm the twelfth, the Midnight Witch—
Let the church bells strike the hour;
Let this potion, sick and sour,
Make men's hearts as black as pitch!

Witch 13
When the clock strikes twelve and one,
The witching hour has begun;
When thirteen hammers hit the bell,
Out come demons out of hell!

Thirteen witches round the pot,
Have all cast in their filthy lot.
Walk the black cat, in reverse,
Thirteen times to seal the curse;
Douse the fire, kill the flame,
So to the pot you do the same;
Now, go forth! Now be seen,
On this night of Halloween!

A Sonnet to The Wolf Man

No gentle man, though good and pure of heart,
Forever faithful, (says his prayer by night),
Can stay the shifting of the wolfbane's dart,
Or keep from baying when the moon is bright.
So bitten, deeply will he feel the pain;
The aching, seething torment of a fire
Which calls the darker side of the insane,
To bear to fore the basest of desire.
So do the throats of those along your path,
Indulge your nature, launch your ripping rage,
And let them feel the burning of your wrath,
Which keeps you slave within your carnal cage.
Embrace the beast, transform yourself, and prowl,
When full the moon, it is your night to howl.

A Terza Rima to the Countess Lefang

Coquette! Vamp! Demonic demimondaine!
Vile mistress of all murky shadows deep;
Seducing fools in misery and pain,

Then striking with a mamba's deadly leap!
So sweet, how well your fangs do cling to lives,
The way a vampire bat does necks of sheep.

Your sharp incisors make such wicked knives,
That quickly sting the flesh, and rip away
The useless human, there attached, who strives

To flee, but hopelessly a price must pay
For presence in unseemly time and place,
But fortunate enough to come your way.

You're heartless, but can hear their pulses race;
A sound that fills your hungry ears with lust,
A joy that puts a light upon your face,

As does the numbered beats that turn to dust
The corpse that will ensue, when flesh has died.
Their deaths is in the nature of your thrust,

So drink, for no one who is dead has cried.

A Rhyming Sestina for the Bride

The Berkeley Mansion is haunted, but it is the old man's
life.
By candlelight, he makes his way to his room,
trying not to disturb his guests, who float and moan.
He's taking a cup of Earl Grey tea to his wife,
to wash away the sorrow and gloom
that soak the mansion, never at peace, never alone.

That's the problem, he thinks, we're never alone
in this place. Why can't they move on to the afterlife?
It's not healthy to live in dreariness and gloom.
Meanwhile, he reaches the master bedroom
and cheerfully says, Happy Anniversary, to his wife,
who, to his attentiveness, lets out a soft moan.

Upon taking a sip of the Earl Grey, another moan
escapes her lips, and she's happy to be alone
with him, husband, wife,
and Earl Grey; alone, at least, in this life,
within the confines of their master bedroom,
for outside of it, the gloom

is too unbearable, the gloom
too pervasive, with ever a ghostly moan
moving spectrally from room to room.
She mutters, why can't they just leave me alone?
At least I can have *some* semblance of life.
Why can't they, all year round, just let me be your wife?

He replies with excitement, tonight they will, my dear
wife!
No sorrow tonight, no sorrow or gloom.
Imagine one more day of life!
Tonight, we won't hear them whisper, or moan.
Tonight we'll have our dance, just you and me, alone!
Come, my love, let us hasten to the living room!

As Mozart's "Minuet" is heard throughout every room
of Berkeley Mansion, the old man dances with his wife.
Finally, this one time of the year, they are alone,
The fog lifted, temporarily the gloom
replaced with joy, no ghostly moan
can be heard, and the couple is thrilled with life.

But in this living room, free of misery and gloom,
Dance a man and his wife, whose bones creak and moan,
For this skeleton, and this skeleton alone, was the love of
his life.

I'm Not Afraid of Creepy Things

I'm not afraid of spiders, bats, or things that creepy crawl
beneath my bed, or up the ivied wall.
I'd merely chase and catch these things, in traps, or in a
jar,
and keep them, if I like, or squash them where they are.
But ghosts are quite a different thing, and never here or
there.
I never know what to expect, it gives me such a scare!

For instance, like I'm bathing, and the curtain's closed all
right,
When suddenly, a creepy shadow moves about the light;
It makes me nearly drown myself, but I don't see
a thing, but soon enough it goes, and soon again I'm me.
Outside of me I am so brave, and act like I don't care,
But way deep, deep inside, it gives me such a scare.

For Instance, by the corners, when I'm walking down the
hall,
From the corner of my eye, I think I see them all.
They hang about the fireplace, or just behind the door,
make footprints on the creaky wood, but soundless on the
floor.
So there I stand, watch, and listen, . . . it's more than I
can bear,
and all my hairs, they stand on end, it gives me such a
scare.

For instance, when the mirrors break, or fog up and perspire,
some words appear upon the glass, ominous and dire.
I wipe away the writing, and much to my surprise,
behind me, for a moment, there's another pair of eyes.
I startle, jump, and turn around, to see if someone's there;
but nothing's there, I pee my pants, it gives me such a scare.
I know you think I'm crazy for there's no such thing as ghosts,
But I am getting out of here, no matter what it costs.
I'll take the snakes and toads and bugs, and everything that crawls;
Heck, I'll even take the creepy things that climb the ivied walls.
And if I die, all scared to death, I'm coming back, I swear,
to walk the halls, and find your bed, to give you such a scare!
BOO!

A Dilemma in A Double Rondelet

I'd like to know:
Which neck's better, blond or brunette?
I'd like to know,
Though necks of redheads steal the show.
Maybe auburn hair's my best bet;
And how tastes silver hair when wet?
I'd like to know!

I'll try them all!
O positive and negative,
I'll try them all!
Mix A and B, and have a ball!
Pass sickle cell blood through a sieve;
And since each neck's got blood to give,
I'll try them all!

A Rondeau to Frankie

He's Frankenstein, a work of art
Who's put together part by part.
Upon his neck, two shiny bolts,
Which may produce ten-thousand volts.
But oh, by gosh, he isn't smart.

He gives the ladies quite a start,
Because their looks are worlds apart.
And sure, we know he has his faults,
He's Frankenstein!

He'll never win a lady's heart,
Unless she's made by counterpart,
With nuts and bolts, electric jolts.
What if she lives, and then revolts?
I'm sure she'll see, that frizzy tart—
He's Frankenstein!

Little Moe Creep

Born in hell, mothered by a witch, little Moe Creep
Loves to sneak around the graveyard stones.
It's what he dreams of when he goes to sleep—
Of corpses, skeletons, and dry, rotting bones,
Which lie beneath the ground, six feet deep.

He has nails, sharp as blades, and two crooked eyes,
Which can see all in darkness, the way bats see the skies;
With hearing acute, he can hear feathers fall,
But his sense of smell is his best sense of all,
For he can smell the aroma of flesh when it dies.

Once has he your scent, he will creep out some night,
To dig, dig, and dig, 'til your coffin's in sight.
Then with some magic word, he will join you inside,
And sincerely thank you before the first bite;
An etiquette, Mother says, fills him with pride.

He will suck out your eyes, bite out your tongue,
Chew off your nails one after another;
Swallow one ear, and then swallow the other,
Or maybe keep one to give to his mother,
But there'll be no more flesh by the time he is done.

Then he'll thank you again, once your bones have dried,
And no one will know he was ever inside.
And if ever he smells you, this little Moe Creep,
Pray that he'll never awaken from sleep,
For he'll dig, dig, dig, dig, and find you — six feet deep!

Spenserian Sonnet to Queen Banshee Eve Aul

Beware the hag, Eve Aul, who hails from lands
Of blood-filled seas, for when the moon is bright,
This Ancient, elf-haired, foxy gray, with hands
Of spindly, sharpened nails, will seize the light,
And in its beams, within the veil of night,
She'll bathe one's corpse in waters cold and deep.
But oh, there will not end this ghastly sight!
Into the ocean, sea, or lake will creep
Your red, for drop by drop, your corpse will weep.
And then your limbs, your hair, your flesh and eyes,
Will wend their way to where the waters sleep,
The fluid tomb where goes the one who dies.
Eve Aul, before this gruesome scene is cast,
Will wail and moan, until you've breathed your last.

Medusa's Love Song

Within Medusa's flesh and bone,
in Stygian darkness tucked away,
there beat a heart of chiseled stone.

It drubbed a song, a Gorgon tone,
in hopes mere mortal men might say
they loved Medusa's flesh and bone.

But no love burned to spark her own;
Athena's curse prevailed each day,
And plagued her heart of chiseled stone.

Then Perseus, son of Zeus, alone,
with shield in hand, had forged a way
to strike Medusa's flesh and bone.

Her writhing locks began to drone,
And hissed the way the vipers pray,
"Pleas-s-s-e, pierce this-s-s heart of chis-s-s-eled s-s
stone."

In slumber's peace, the sword struck home;
No longer would she swish and sway.
In death Medusa's flesh and bone,
Had loved her chiseled heart of stone.

A Triolet to a Vampire's Immortality

You must be bitten by a vampire
If you wish to be immortal.
To feel the ice and free the fire,
You must be bitten by a vampire.
Only then will you claim your heart's desire,
Having passed through the graveyard portal.
But first, be smitten by a vampire
If you truly wish to be immortal.

The Death of Karetta Tress

The evil Lord Na-Tass, one moonless night,
From deep within the flames that Helkron wrought,
Flung forth a fearsome phantom spurred by light
That to the cradle maiden loins have brought.
Too late, when gone, a mother's soul's delight,
That nine months kept in womb then proves has naught.
For when a child not blessed by water sleeps:
The spirit thief Karetta Tress there creeps!

But Jaho Vesh, great Lord of Haven-Or,
Sent forth the mighty wizer Axxon Thorn
To slay the demon lesser men abhor.
Within her den, by sacred sword well worn,
Her heart was pierced and from the body torn.
In Helkron's fires Karetta Tress will creep,
Lest mothers fail to bless their little souls to sleep!

Here Comes the Boggelbugge!

You are tucked in bed, the covers drawn,
Your heart is racing towards the break of dawn!
Boggelbugge, Boogeyman, Bogeyman, boo!
The closet door creaks, batteries dead,
Wild are the images inside your head!
Boggelbugge, Boogeyman, Bogeyman, boo!
Something's creeping, you're grabbed, and you scream—
AAAHHH!
You disappear into a wicked dream!
Boggelbugge . . . Boogeyman . . . Bogeyman—BOO!

The Mummy's Curse

From the Book of the Dead, read not,
Lest you bring a curse upon your head!
The words there spoken will bring you dread,
If Imhotep rises with his wicked lot.

Anck su-Namun, in a lover's knot,
Killed the Pharaoh, and Imhotep fled.
Better to shirk this murderous plot,
Than to bring a curse upon your head.

So, buried alive, he was left to rot,
To join the souls of the evil dead.
(Where better forgotten than to stir his bed)
Imhotep's tomb will be a hidden spot,
If, from the Book of the Dead—you read not!

The Frankenstein Monster

There is death within the tower where it lives,
Though life's been given by the currents of the skies.
The very same that Heaven to a creature gives,
Mustn't be disturbed when such a creature dies.

Too many souls, in parts, one soul deceives;
And in its mind, there is a hateful flood of lies.
Great is death within the tower where it lives,
Though life has given it the currents of the skies.

If the Creator such creator's sin forgives,
And the sin itself is pitied when it cries,
Absolution may be most what man receives,
If repentance dwells in sin's and sinner's eyes.
To this death, within the tower where it lives,
Its life be taken swiftly by the currents of the skies.

Halloween Haiku

a ghost's kiss; sweetly,
then I wept — for though I slept
she touched me deeply

howling through the trees
chills my spine, freezes my mind
hear my rattling knees

beware the Banshee
pitiful moans, gruesome groans
deadly is her plea

lycanthropic Moon
what is within turns without
death inopportune

creaking closet door
heart resounding pulse pounding
pleasant dream no more

you do and you don't
see you will but see you won't
rowdy poltergeists

fangs of the vampire
slowly sink, death on the brink
jugular on fire

Halloween pumpkin
saw-toothed sharp-eyed demon's head
Hell's candle within

fire's vitality
icy-cold siphoning fangs
immortality

footprints on the floor
murder mystery unfolds
blood from under door

lady's soft shadow
tumultuous agony
buried alive beau

wintry corridor
hissing pussycat breaks out
goblins at the door

quick hirsute prowler
horrendous pains breaking chains
silver moon howler

Halloween observed
one human at the party
soon dinner is served

no invitation
(vampire knocking at your door)
your one salvation

nearer and nearer
face to face and out of place
nothing in mirror

one amorous fool
the other only loves flesh
fangs sharp and cruel

black widow in red
suitor trembling at her door
hanging by a thread

on my neck hot breath
guttural emanations
holding hands with Death

coffin six feet deep
a somber awakening
from a heavy sleep

graveyard escapade
rattling bones through the headstones
essence of Night Shade

candlelight dinner
hunger pangs too great for fangs
widowed web spinner

Fright Night

If Hell is where Beelzebub resides,
What creature moves blood-curdling scream and moan?
It must be demons he has sent to roam
the land, as well as spooks for shores besides.
The belfry, or the coffin, either hides
the Demon Bat, while graveyards are the home
of other sorts, like ghouls and ghosts, who hone
their skills on fears of men, by leaps and strides.
However, there's one night when all come out—
The gremlins and the goblins, good and bad,
While witches, and the warlocks, romp about
In search of mischief, always to be had.
But nothing can compare to evil seen,
When humans all come out on Halloween.

A Douzet From the Werewolf

I am a wolf, now come and hear me howl,
And let me send such shivers down your spine
That all your nightmares will appear divine
When I am at your neck with spit and growl.

I'll tear your throat, for that is what I do,
But way before I bite, you'll long be dead
From fright more than from severing of head;
And that is all the kindness I'll give you.

So wary be, when I am on the prowl.
I've no forgiveness in this soul of mine,
For I must do what Hell and Heaven said,
And that is to my nature to be true.

The Devil's Blood Violin

Some time ago, outside of Rome, a beggar, blind, bereft of
home,
Walked the streets in rags, alone; he owned one blood-red
violin.
This violin, of blesséd strings, it sang the way an angel
sings;
Its notes, aloft on silken wings, had soothed my ears and
soul within.
Oh, how those notes, on silken wings, had touched my
heart and soul within!
I felt . . . as if absolved of sin.

I contemplated, to possess, such implement of loftiness,
For in my craft, I must confess, I had not risen very well.
But with a tool so pure, divine, I knew success could soon
be mine
If, all at once, I could align with such a tool that casts a
spell—
Such *instrument* which casts such spells, to dare one
walk the flames of Hell,
 So none, such craft, can parallel!

I sought, and met, this beggar man, in hopes of progress
with my plan,
Where from those blesséd notes began, where he played
so marvelously.
I begged his pardon and he ceased, and not at all was he
displeased.
The contrary, he seemed quite pleased I took his playing

65

seriously.
His blind hand sought out mine, and then, so chilling and
so odd was he,
He quietly laughed deliriously.

"Maestro Vitale, glad you came," he said, as if to curse
my name.
"This violin will bring you fame, it only needs your
sacred soul."
"Will you take of gold or silver?" Dared I ask, with oddly
shiver,
"This, to you, I can deliver, and thereby keep my spirit
whole."
"There's nothing else will it appease," said he, "but that
you take control!"
I swear, I heard a death knell toll!

Not long it took me to succeed, where coin and fame
became my greed,
And failed to see the ugly seed that sprouted out such
ugly fruit!
For when one decade then had passed, and all my glories
I'd amassed,
The strings detuned and then harassed me 'til I wished to
make them mute.
I tried to mute the violin, but it was never rendered mute.
It was a frivolous pursuit.

Although I tried no more to play, the violin would have
its way;
By some demonic pull and sway, I couldn't foil its
strange allure.

I had to play it, day and night, although I tried, with all my might,
To take a wrong and make it right, by smashing such a thing un-pure!
Instead I played, and played, and played, and like a madman, I am sure!
I knew, alas, there'd be no cure.

The beggar man, to my surprise, appeared in offense to my eyes;
And with a laughter I despise, I saw that he had seen quite well.
He'd seen what was inside of me, knew what it was I was to be,
So came he to collect his fee, and make me hence his infidel;
And not enough, he took my sight, and cast me to where now I dwell—
Upon the streets of my own hell.

So now this Violin I play, wherein, my dreaded fears betrayed,
I cannot help but shake, and pray, yes, for my revindication.
For the time has finally run, to wit, amends for deeds I'd done,
There, once for all, the pact, he'd won, sealing sure my soul's damnation.
Clearly put, I'd lost; he'd won, succinctly, by interpretation.
May my death be my salvation.

But be informed, until I die, discordant are the notes I
ply,
Though blissfully they seem to fly, they're but a ruse and
nothing more!
So sweetly sound they in your head, but they are coarse
to bring you dread,
By waking demons out of bed, and all your nightmares
there outpour!
Ungodly, ghastly, ghostly nightmares will pursue you
theretofore!
So heed my warning—hear no more!

The Ballad of the Invisible Man

Jim Hotep loved Ann Oksana Moon,
The Invisible Man's lady and bride.
Two star-crossed lovers who didn't see
The folly of their passionate side.

CHORUS:
Well you can't see what you cannot see,
And there's really no place to hide,
When lurking about, the transparent man,
May be standing right by your side, your side,
May be standing right by your side.

One day, Oksana Moon said, give it a go,
And do in this glassy eyed gent.
So Jim agreed to her bidding do,
Until missing man's life be spent.

CHORUS

The Invisible Man, all neatly wrapped up,
In his living room he could be seen,
Surrounded in threads like a mummy would,
Looking so dapper and keen.

CHORUS

Jim Hotep waited, and saw his chance,
His knife found its target true.
He stabbed the Invisible Man where he sat,
The blood gushing out into view.

CHORUS

Then suddenly, Jim, felt a dagger himself,
And realized the wickedness done.
Wrapped like a mummy was Oksana Moon,
And the Invisible Man had won.

Well you can't see what you cannot see,
And there's really no place to hide,
When lurking about, the Invisible Man,
May be standing right by your side, your side,
May be standing right by your side.

Rondeau Redoublé From Lady Blayne to Count Lefang

I know the risk, and I'll not disagree,
Inside me there's a flame you understand.
It is a fire for immortality,
The mightiness to life and death command.

Soon my own life will be yours to demand
And you may wield this force to set me free.
I do not hesitate, I give my hand,
And know the risk, so I'll not disagree.

I've thought it many hours, silently,
When whispers from your mind to mine expand.
You must know then my heart, and plain to see
Inside me, there's a flame you understand.

Do not condemn me to the depths of land,
For, yes, I also sense your cruelty.
I'll say this was exactly what we planned,
To sate my fire for immortality.

It is as if we were designed to be,
From death, two ends of one whole single strand,
To wield the change, pursue then savagely,
The mightiness to life and death command.

And we will storm and rage, in ways so grand,
Until the end of our eternity.
I yield, aforethought, as companion, and
I bare myself to you, so heed my plea;
I know the risk.

Ballade to The Vamp Lady Blayne

So recently, poor Blayne, deceased,
Was quickly to her tomb addressed.
But others swore she was released
By some unholy rite unblessed,
To take a new and earthly quest
To empty each and every vein
of all the drops which therein rest.
Who should be pitied more than Blayne?

Her tomb, discovered, had been fleeced
Of what at one time had been blessed.
The hounds, low growling, were unleashed
To hunt this wickedness possessed
Of appetite so cruel at best,
You could not call it but profane,
And should be, from this world, expressed.
Who should be pitied more than Blayne?

The hunters heard the hounds, displeased,
And towards the howls the hunters pressed.
They found the bodies, blood decreased,
That Blayne had added to her nest;
It showed the nature in her breast,
And was by cross and fire then slain,
Which ended her poor soul's unrest.
Who should be pitied more than Blayne?

If by the vampire I am stressed,
Then take my life and ease my pain.
For then I'll be one, put to test,
Who should be pitied more than Blayne.

Ballade to the Bride of Frankenstein

The deed is done, they've built, anew, one more—
A creature fair for such an unfair groom.
Your parts, collected from the graveyard gore,
Can only bring you hell from certain doom,
For though you live, your cheeks lack rosy bloom.
But not to blame, yourself, so innocent,
For earthly godsmen to such deeds are bent,
To flirt with Nature, and then bend her still,
To forge a damsel not by Heaven sent.
Oh, scream, my Lady, scream, with voice to kill!

What are you now that you were not before?
Together put, like quilt to perk a room,
Tell, what will fate for you now have in store?
You love not it who loves you most! Such gloom,
And dire days, your whole life will consume.
If left unloved, then better life be spent,
Before your love and life you both lament.
Since you were brought to life against your will,
Against your will your spirit will be rent.
Oh, scream, my Lady, scream, with voice to kill!

All must be turned to right as was afore,
For all your peaceful nights to reassume;
Seek out the spark that through your bosom bore,
And let the fires of all your anger fume,
Until once more you rest within your tomb.
As for your makers, fire was also meant;
If all their deeds they wish not to relent,

Then by all heavenly, angelic skill,
They're ever damned if they do not repent.
Oh, scream, my Lady, scream, with voice to kill!

Whatever fleeting moments life has lent,
They are not yours, and kept, they will torment
Your very soul; so scream, and scream, until,
Your very silence proves your life outspent.
Yes, scream, my Lady, scream, with voice to kill!

Double Ballad of the Wicked Pumpkin King

In the land of the scarecrows, the corn-filled plain,
Where the savage wind throws its breath to and fro,
They say works a figure, cruel and insane,
Who tends a garden where special things grow,
The things made of nightmares you don't want to know;
Some that take over your mental estate,
So even your daydreams have nowhere to go.
From the Pumpkin King, run, before it's too late!

If you dare travel there, then your will be fain!
Else he'll wither your mind when his eyes are aglow,
So your heart may suffer the strife you'll gain,
And your body be buried in his garden of woe,
Along with the others, like stalks in a row!
Long will you fester there, flower of hate,
So heed now this warning, I'll whisper it low:
From the Pumpkin King, run, before it's too late!

But should your misfortune rest in his domain,
He'll dig, gently bury you, water, and sow
The seed of your fears, on your face a stain,
Where, no love lost, his own eyes will show,
Your own dead soul in the deeps below.
Where are you, then, but in the hands of fate!
Will you awaken? How will you know?
From the Pumpkin King, run, before it's too late!

Oh, he is the master of agony and pain,
And you his flower to be picked before snow.

His scythe will cut like the pitiless rain,
Through your struggling neck, and its bloody flow,
Whereto, your life, will seem long, long ago,
Gone to the lands where the angels await,
But hell is more likely your spirit to throw.
From the Pumpkin King, run, before it's too late!

He'll sit and sing a macabre refrain,
While your eyelids flicker, sadly and slow;
And a blade, on your skull, with struggle and strain,
Carves out a pattern that many will know.
With eye sockets hollowed, calling friend and foe,
All will empathize with your stress so great,
That they'll say to themselves, as they come and go,
From the Pumpkin King, run, before it's too late!

A candle will brighten you, skull and no brain,
And through eyes, and teeth, that light will glow;
On a porch, or deck, or through a window pane,
You'll find no heaven towards which to grow.
You've lived your past, and given up tomorrow,
There's nothing left to do but wait
For those who've lost all hope, and tell it so:
From the Pumpkin King, run? It's too late, too late!

Double Refrain Ballad of the Scarecrow of Creepy Hollow

If you happen to stray on Halloween night,
Where the gold Harvest Moon eerily glows,
Amidst the stalks, filled with tallness and fright,
You'll find yourself kin to the corn that grows.
Chilled is the spine when the North Wind blows,
But chillier still is the guardian of sorrow;
And fed be your flesh to the magpies and crows,
By the hand of the Scarecrow of Creepy Hollow.

If you find you're mired in your Halloween plight,
And stuck in the land where nobody goes,
The nightmare is real, and though hardy your fight,
You'll find yourself kin to the corn that grows.
Planted, you've root of your painful throes,
Where maggots and worms your legs seek to borrow;
And though death may you wish, your life still flows
By the hand of the Scarecrow of Creepy Hollow.

If you're screaming for help with all of your might,
Be not ever surprised if no one shows,
For though you have hopes of seeing the light,
You'll find yourself kin to the corn that grows.
As your flesh turns black, like the withering rose,
And your bones reach upward, sturdy and sallow,
You've been sent to the grave where wickedness goes,
By the hand of the Scarecrow of Creepy Hollow.

Who've all lost their way, have tallied their woes—
And found themselves kin to the corn that grows

In the fields of death,—where graves are shallow,
By the hand of the Scarecrow of Creepy Hollow.

A Rhyme Royal from the Black Widow

They come to me, all they who think me weak.
With beauty's red, I lure them to my lair.
So willingly they come to kiss my cheek,
When perfume sweet I spill into the air,
That danger seems of no concern to bear;
And in my hands, so secretively strange,
So subtly, they know soon enough my change.

My pouting lips, you'll find not otherwise,
A thousand times more sweet than honey mead;
With slender form, which Venus may despise,
You cannot help but go where I will lead,
Where what you crave is often what I need.
While in your arms, I'll simply ask you this:
"How do you recognize a fatal kiss?"

But realizing means it's far too late,
For all is turned away from gentleness;
When passion, onto passion, seals our fate,
There's nothing that will make my poison less,
Or steal you from impending wickedness.
So if you seek, then I will surely serve,
So both of us may get what we deserve.

The Death of the Demon Captain Ben Gravely

'Twas summer of seventeen-fifty-three—
The Iv'ry Coast turned an ebony sea.
Man Cager, well laden with flesh, set sail
To the rattle of chains, and: "Wail! Wind wail!"

The captain, Ben Gravely, master of pain,
Each shadow thrashed he, again and again!
All thought him a ghost so wicked and pale,
As he prayed to the Devil, "Wail! Wind wail!"

All dark flesh puckered out gashes of red—
So shot were the eyes in Ben Gravely's head.
Oh, how brown limbs struggled to no avail,
For their chains kept clamoring, "Wail! Wind wail!"

Princes of Abidjan kneeled down to cry
For Princesses raked by the Devil's eye.
They prayed for the breath of a mighty gale
To steal from the captain his, "Wail! Wind wail!"

And Princesses wept, both deeply and well,
For their flesh was bound to the core of Hell!
No mercy was given by lust or ale,
As long as Ben Gravely yelled, "Wail! Wind wail!"

Soon clouds of seagulls flew over the main
While sharks made frenzy to their wild refrain.
Dark freedom stripped like the blubber of whale
Brought cheers from the crew and a, "Wail! Wind wail!"

Then a chant arose like a Panther's growls,
A roar far greater than the wind that howls!
Captain and crew were all thrust to the rail,
And from sea to sky they heard, "Wail! Wind wail!"

The skies grew darker than bile of a witch,
Man Cager cracked under tossing and pitch!
Over the crew ran a darkening veil,
While the Iv'ry Coast chanted, "Wail! Wind wail!"

To the briny deep fell cargo and crew,
Where the Devil waited to claim his due;
The churning waters, and an angry gale,
Silenced, forever, Gravely's, "Wail, wind wail!"

The Devil took Gravely, sharks took the rest.
'Twas a day all men were put to the test;
And alone I survived to tell this tale,
And if death means freedom, well then, "Wail! Wind!
WAIL!"

An Ogre's Complaint

I'm often called, Neanderthal,
But Ogre's what I am.
When I go out the people shout
And take it on the lam.

In my defense, and no offense,
The folks here are so rude.
Now don't they know—I love them so?
That's why they are pursued.

I'm not Cyclops, who loves lamb chops,
Nor witch who children bakes;
And you have proof, I'm not the Wolf
Who Red for Granny takes.

I'm just a guy who has an eye
For all the human good.
Good legs, good arms, and other charms,
The way good ogres should.

Folks are so sweet; they always beat
The gaming, farming kind,
That I do swear, on days so rare,
I keep them off my mind.

To be exact, it is a fact,
I'm just a hungry brute;
And you will see, I'm being me,
Next time I'm in pursuit!

Dining With Death

There came a visitor called Death,
All dressed in black and purple shade,
With staff tipped with a sharpened blade,
And curved to cut well through the air.
There came a visitor called Death—
When I was driven towards despair.

There was no point to take his hand,
Nor sense to visit his dark land,
For I still breathed, though out of breath.
He must have known, I know, and still,
He came, this visitor called Death.
His book has pages yet to fill,
Which I help fill, each day, each year,
And this it was which brought him here.

For dinner, many guests I keep,
And sometimes I do overeat,
Much to the bad, I cannot sleep,
But sated, they are out of breath.
I'm very bad with names, I fear . . .
But not my visitor called Death!
He writes them down, all nice and neat,
Each day, each month, year after year.
So by my fangs I must invite
My friend called, Death, home for a bite.

Haunted Oaks and Weeping Willows

A walk through the Oaks or the Weeping Willows,
Which path is more filled with fright,
If the headstones are strewn between the two
And the moon is full and bright?

If the Oaks are tall, and barren their boughs,
Their shadows bring shudders to bear,
While phantoms appear to move through the dark,
To raise every strand of my hair.

I move, and they move, the arms of the Oaks,
Then I hope the wind is to blame,
But the wind blows not, not a whisper is heard,
And I shiver away just the same.

So fancy and free, the wind then decides
To scurry the leaves about,
The sound seems like burning around my feet,
And I'm anxious to take them out.

The moon is no help, casting slivers of light,
Through the Weeping Willows I'm led.
Their sighs, their moans, their whispering noise,
Are like voices to stir up the dead.

Are they speaking to me, I say to myself,
Do they want me to hear and reply.
Most certain, I am, they would call out my name
Were I, at that moment, to die.

Then it dawns on me, why these Willows all weep,

And these Oak Trees are filled with hate;
And a reason why this graveyard is full,
For many have passed through its gate.

Long, long ago, both guilty and guiltless,
More guiltless than guilty I know,
Were hanged from the boughs of these mighty Oaks,
And left there to swing to and fro.

Much sooner than later, a man hangs still,
Or a lady quits kicking her heels;
And many a soul hang on to the bark
To tell the poor Oak how it feels.

So an Oak gets mad, for it feels the pain
Of an innocent soul that dies;
And a Willow can't help its empathy,
So the Willow breaks down and cries.

If you walk this walk then it's crystal clear
Which path is more laden with fright:
It's the path that winds through heartless men,
Such men . . . who frighten the trees at night.

Saving Bloody Mary

Mirror, mirror, mirror—make your face a portal;
Let this vessel, in her place, stare the glassy frame,
And let pass, who is a ghost, but was once a mortal.
Now, by candle, in the dark, thrice be called her name:

Mary, Mary, Mary come, do your wretched worst.
If you were unjustly tried, no longer will you weep;
Come and honor here your last, those you rightly cursed,
For you've much to settle here, and promises to keep.

Body mine be yours to hold until you feel absolved
Of all your wrongful sins, to find you peace at last;
And in so doing, lose the curse, leaving all resolved,
Then take the glass, go home, and know your pain has
passed.

Dr. Henry Jekyll and Mr. Edward Hyde

Duality's the nature of a man
Where angels and the demons fight the war.
Each one intent on topping out the score:
The demons seek to topple Heaven's plan,
The angels look to save the souls they can.
Two sides, one soul, which end will claim the fight?
One side the day, the other side the night,
Whichever lands on top, they both will lose,
For Nature, day or night, it cannot choose—
When both must be of one to make things right.
But Man has will to turn him towards the light,
Or at the very least, a balance made
Between the two, for if one is betrayed,
No Heaven can the two then reunite.

Arachnophilia

To have eight legs, I think it would be nice,
With silken thread to hang from place to place.
I'd love to dangle upside down, or race
Across my trampoline, with steps precise,
And sticky feet, towards prey my webs entice.
I'd be a Jumper, and a Trap Door too,
Or maybe a Tarantula would do.
Like Daddy Longlegs, I could travel far,
Or like the Wolf, scare people from afar.
For sure, the Parson would advise me to
Be careful of what Widow I may woo.
But I would love my poisoned fangs the most,
To sink them in my unsuspecting host,
Then draw out every drop of human goo.

Not Death Us Do Part

I met her at the *Wicked Bar and Grill,*
And Witches Brew, I fear, was sure to blame,
That I did woo and wed that vibrant flame;
But soon enough, I found her looks could kill,
To which, I took an axe to her good will.
But neither depth nor dirt will keep her dead,
For when the sun goes down, she finds my bed!
It wouldn't be a fix if I were drunk,
But she has come back smelling like a skunk—
Plus bad enough, her breath does ache my head!
Her wormy skin is orange, black, and red,
So squishy to the lightest, slightest touch,
That I beseech you, thank you very much,
To kill me should I choose again to wed!

The Night Johnny Jilted Ophelia

Ophelia, jilted by her fiancé,
Heartbrokenly distraught, she took the cliff.
Surprised, she found herself a walking stiff,
And climbed the very rocks she leapt that day,
To seek the scoundrel who would have to pay.
When Johnny saw her, he was filled with fright,
But then he saw she was a silly sight.
With one eye popped, a crooked shin, an ear
lopped off, and broken teeth—she looked so queer,
That Johnny couldn't help, with all his might,
The laughing fit that filled him with delight.
Oh, she got mad, and dragged him to the edge,
And tossed him over that old rocky ledge.
Well, there's a couple for Halloween night!

When the Night Wind Howls

As oaks, with arms outstretched, embrace the night,
The cold wind howls across a sea of stones;
Two thugs, who carry there a bag of bones,
In silence, walk to where the moon gives light.
Much ugly mischief is afoot tonight,
To dig a grave and cast a body there,
A body, once, so innocent and fair.
But jilted lovers often vengeance crave,
And quittance may arrive from out the grave.
The jilting lover, with a devious flair,
Affirms he's innocent of this affair.
But when the night wind howls, and truth be told,
Retortion moves the earth to serve it cold,
And Innocence, this night, will claim her fare!

Waking the Warlock Tolodo

Oh wicked one, of deepest, darkest night:
O ve, nami bru, que ja, nami vu,
Haz que lo, yo te, no te, lo que tu!
Send your familiar in absence of light!
I have a conjurin' to do tonight!
Tolodo, que pi, es do, al haz, que may,
Pi que Tolodo, odolot,—obey!
From corpse the fat you'll eat so you can fly—
Un-baptized, from his head I plucked his eye!
But first, this charm will help you find your way!
To me! And listen well to what I say:
O ve nami bru que ja vooni oy,
Haz que tu dolopi telo que toy!
Come Tolodo, Tolodo come, —obey!

Don't Be Afraid of the Dark

There's nothing there, but something's there alright,
A shadow cast by coats upon a rack,
A noise a house may make to stretch its back,
And even scratching nails of rats at night
Can chill a bone, and fill a soul with fright.
But in the mind, a coat's a ghost of lore;
The howling wind—a Banshee at your door!
Beneath your bed, your shoes tap out a dance,
And just outside your room, the goblins prance!
But worse, your closet has the worst in store,
With creaking hinges sounding like a roar!
Inside, a host of demons set to pounce,
Such demons, all whose names you won't pronounce,
For if you're wrong, you'll scream, then scream some
more!

The Coffin in My Cellar

She oddly died, not long ago, and I,
Who should have better known, here must confess,
I did the worst, and kept my lovely Tess
At home, to keep my love forever nigh.
But then one night, I thought I heard her cry.
A ghastly sound beyond my cellar door,
A horrid screech I never heard before,—
Engulfed my senses, chilled my heart and soul!
Much so, my shaking I could not control.
A horrid crash from underneath the floor,
And through the wood this demon creature bore!
Without so much as by-your-leave it came,
A bat-like voice screamed out, and called my name,
And now I die— for I can scream no more!

The Apparition

I know I drowned her, days ago, I swear,
But I don't think she's up to staying down,
And I do fear—I feel her still around!
When creaks the floor, I think I see her there,
But in a blink, her countenance is air.
I cannot rest by day, nor sleep by night,
And on and off and on she flips the light!
So wary I must be of flights of stairs,
Of knives, of nails, of blades, of flying chairs!
If I decide to eat, my hand she'll bite,
If I go left, she knocks me to the right!
I try to rest, and lie down on my bed,
But next you know, I'm standing on my head!
Hey! If I drown myself, then fair the fight!

The Frankenstein Conflict

I am . . . a puzzle built of human parts,
A riddle Doctor Frankenstein has made.
For am I one or multiple displayed?
Have I a heart that beats the many hearts?
And lose I soul or souls when life departs?
Has Doctor-god, from God, incurred his wrath?
Do I have rights to the celestial path?
I think, as one, so I have unity,
With feelings of my own mortality,
And therefore, I am real, and not a sham;
And I may be a being God may damn.
So I must isolate myself, for good,
And beg, for both, forgiveness, as I should,
For all my thoughts say: I . . . am who . . . I am.

The Talking

I

I hear the people talking—
Children talking!
Oh, what nonsense in palaver keeps them squawking!
Instead of dying—people talking, talking, talking,
Children talking!
While I, in jacket, snug and tight,
In my jacket oh so bright,
In my room of pads, of brightest white,
Lost in some forever time,
Adrift of reason, lost of rhyme,
With great exacerbation hear the talking,
All the talking, talking, talking,
And more talking, talking, talking,
Exasperating, aggravating, irritating talking!

II

Hear, again, the foolish, boorish talking,
Addleheaded talking!
What a world of monstrous, empty-headed balking!
Through the day, until the night,
How they nag, and whine, and fight!
Throughout the house, from every room,
How I long to hear KA-BOOM!
To kill the record, broken, out of tune,
And send them to the moon!
Oh, how sandy sounds the talking,
What a gush voluminous of loggerheaded talking!
Nails on blackboard talking!
Pencil-in-my-ear-like talking!

Ad infinitum, am I doomed to hear the talking?
The staggering and daggering
Of their talking, talking, talking,
Of the scheming, streaming, screaming of their
talking?

III
No longer will I bear the pounding of their talking—
The caterwaulers talking!
What tale of terror, now, I've got for all their talking!
When in they settle for the night
How they'll scream out all in fright!
They'll be horrified to speak,
They will only shriek and shriek,
Wrecked and out of tune, like a loony, loony, loon!
I can feel it in my mind, all my homicidal fire,
Heading towards one massive and explosive feat of
ire,
That will take me higher, higher, higher,
To my desperate desire,
Of much stillness . . . now and ever,
Now—now, now, and forever,
To kill the record, broken, out of tune,
And send them packing to the moon!
How the people talking, talking, talking,
Children talking,
All will end, and what tale they'll tell
When in despair, I send them shredded all to hell!
How my ear will laud the silence,
All my madness then in balance,
Without the twanging,
Or the banging.
How my ears, the blissful muteness,

Will then soften my vile bruteness,
With no jangling,
Or the wrangling,
No more stinking people talking, talking, talking—
No children talking—
No one talking, talking, talking, talking,
Talking, talking, talking—
No more clinking, stinking talking, talking, talking!

IV
Hear the death knell tolling of the bells—
As I'm freed, hear the deleterious ringing of the bells!
When the people cease their talking,
Children stop their talking, talking,
But can't sleep, then the terror speaks in swells!
I'll wait inside the closet, in the silence of the night,
How I'll make them quake, and shiver with such
fright.
When all is dark, and the doorknob squeaks a turn,
How such nightmares in their minds will burn!
Slowly will I push the creaking door,
I'll make it creak, and make it creak some more!
They'll tremble when the creaking floats,
And catches words within their throats,
And then I'll groan.
No longer will I bear the hounding of their talking—
The imbecilic talking!
What tale of horror, now, they'll get for all their
talking!
In the stillness of the night
How they'll scream with all their might!
They'll be horrified to speak,
They will only shriek and shriek,

Wrecked and out of tune, like a loony, loony, loon!
And the children—ah, the people—
Like a church bell in the steeple,
They'll be all alone.
How their teeth will chatter, chatter, chatter,
With a voice all their own,
And I'll love the clatter, clatter, clatter,
While I turn a heart to stone.
Be it child, a man, or woman,
They'll soon know I am not human—
I am the Boggelbugge!
Now, NO MORE TALKING!

Treat 'r Trick

The thing I like 'bout Halloween
Is I can walk around unseen,
Underneath a wicked veil,
Leaving 'hind a bloody trail!

CHORUS
Treat or trick, treat or trick, doesn't matter what I
pick.
Treat or trick, treat or trick, rotten candy makes me
sick.

I've got candy strychnine laced,
For the treater angel-faced,
Arsenic will also do,
For the tricker just like you!

CHORUS

Pumpkinhead is tall and mean,
Creeper's sense of smell is keen,
Boogeyman's a closet creep,
Doesn't like to let you sleep!

CHORUS

Freddie Kruger haunts your dreams,
Jason never dies it seems,
Bloody Mary is so hot,
When her cleaver hits the spot!

CHORUS

Strangers kill because they can,
Hitcher's not a lady's man,
Peeping Tom's a cinch to peek,
Charlie likes his hide and seek.

CHORUS

Blade the puppetmaster's whack
ChromeSkull's face is hard to crack,
Mr. Brooks kills with finesse,
Jack the Ripper leaves a mess.

CHORUS

Pinhead likes to raise some hell,
Pumpkin Karver carves so well,
Killer Clause kills Christmas Eve,
Madman Marz has skulls to cleave.

CHORUS

Candyman has one mean hook,
Hatchet hates the way you look,
Carrie really wrecked the prom,
Killed her classmates and her mom!

CHORUS

Michael Meyers hates his kin,
Leatherface gives chains a spin,
Ghostface likes to grab and stab,
Chucky likes to jab and jab!

CHORUS

Jigsaw has his traps that kill,
Hannibal has Buff'lo Bill,
Tooth Fairy is awf'ly nice,
Knocks your teeth out twice or thrice!

CHORUS

Trick or treat, trick or treat,
Please be careful what you eat.
Treat or trick, treat or trick,
Rotten candy makes you sick!

HAPPY HALLOWEEN!

Some of Count Lefang's Favorite Movie Antagonists

Blade (Puppetmaster – 1989)
Bloody Mary (Bloody Mary – 2006)
Boogeyman (Boogeyman – 2005)
Candyman (Candyman – 1992)
Carrie (Carrie – 1976)
Charlie (Hide and Seek – 2005)
ChromeSkull (Laid to Rest – 2009)
Chucky (Child's Play – 1988)
Creeper (Jeepers Creepers – 2001)
Freddie Kruger (Nightmare on Elm Street – 1984)
Ghostface (Scream – 1996)
Hannibal (Silence of the Lambs – 1991)
Hatchet (Hatchet – 2006)
Hitcher (The Hitcher – 1986)
Jack the Ripper (From Hell – 2001)
Jason (Friday the 13th – 1980)
Jigsaw (Saw – 2004)
Killer Clause (Silent Night, Deadly Night – 1984)
Leatherface (Texas Chainsaw Massacre – 1974)
Madman Marz (Madman – 1982)
Michael Meyers (Halloween – 1978)
Mr. Brooks (Mr. Brooks – 2007)
Peeping Tom (Peeping Tom – 1960)
Pinhead (Hellraiser – 1987)
Pumpkinhead (Pumpkinhead – 1988)
Pumpkin Karver (Pumpkin Karver – 2006)
Strangers (The Strangers – 2008)
Tooth Fairy (Darkness Falls – 2003)